W9-BNN-607

I Like to Draw!
CARS
and
TRUCKS

by Rochelle Baltzer   Illustrated by James Penfield

Looking Glass Library
An Imprint of Magic Wagon
www.abdopublishing.com

www.abdopublishing.com

Published by Magic Wagon, a division of ABDO, PO Box 398166, Minneapolis, Minnesota 55439. Copyright © 2015 by Abdo Consulting Group, Inc. International copyrights reserved in all countries. No part of this book may be reproduced in any form without written permission from the publisher. Looking Glass Library™ is a trademark and logo of Magic Wagon.

Printed in the United States of America, North Mankato, Minnesota.
102014
012015

Cover and Interior Elements and Photos: iStockphoto, Thinkstock

Written by Rochelle Baltzer
Illustrations by James Penfield
Edited by Megan M. Gunderson, Bridget O'Brien
Cover and interior design by Candice Keimig

Library of Congress Cataloging-in-Publication Data

Baltzer, Rochelle, 1982– author.
  Cars and trucks / written by Rochelle Baltzer ; illustrated by James Penfield.
      pages cm. -- (I like to draw!)
  Includes index.
  ISBN 978-1-62402-080-3
1. Automobiles in art--Juvenile literature. 2. Trucks in art--Juvenile literature. 3. Drawing--Technique--Juvenile literature. I. Penfield, James, illustrator. II. Title.
  NC825.A8B35 2015
  743.8'96292--dc23
                          2014034577

TABLE of CONTENTS

CARS and TRUCKS

Have you ever seen a really awesome car or truck you wanted to draw? There are many different kinds of cars and trucks. Some are built for racing around tight curves. Others are **equipped** with special tools, such as a ladder and a hose for firefighting. Let's draw some cool cars and trucks!

STUFF YOU'LL NEED

Pencil

Paper

Eraser

Marker

Colored Pencils

KNOW THE BASICS

SHAPES

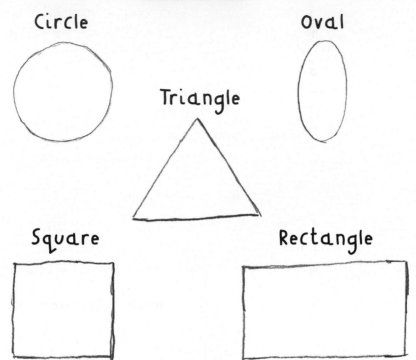

Circle

Oval

Triangle

Square

Rectangle

LINES
thick & thin

Straight

Wavy

Jagged

TALK LIKE AN ARTIST

Composition

Composition is the way parts of a drawing or picture are arranged. Balanced composition means having an even amount of parts, such as lines and shapes.

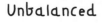

Unbalanced

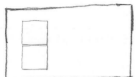

Balanced

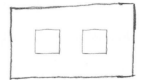

Dimension

Dimension is the amount of space an object takes up. Drawings are created on a flat surface and have length and width but not depth. So, they are two-dimensional. You can give an object depth by layering colors and adding shadow. This makes it look like it's popping off the page!

Without Dimension

With Dimension

Shadow

Shadow is created by the way light shines on an object. Look outside on a sunny day. See how the sunlight shines on a tree? The side of the tree with more sunlight appears lighter than the other side.

Without Shadow

With Shadow

VINTAGE CAR

Do you know what a vintage car looks like? These old cars are long and sit low to the ground. Built from 1919 through 1930, vintage cars have large, round headlights. The spare tire is often mounted on the side of the car. The Cadillac V16 is one popular vintage car introduced in 1930.

1 Draw two rectangles for the body of the car and four circles for the tires.

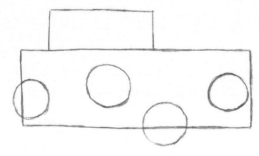

2 Add five small ovals for the headlights. Draw shapes for the front windshield and side window.

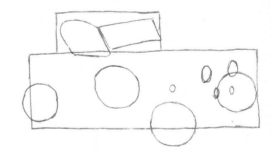

3 Outline the body of the car. Add two rearview mirrors. Add details to the tires and lights.

4 Further detail the body and tires. Add a seat, steering wheel, and rear window to the interior.

ART TIP

If you put in extra time at the beginning of a drawing to get your shapes correct, the final piece will look balanced and realistic.

5 Outline the finished drawing with a thin, black marker.

6 Pick a dark, rich color for this vintage car to give it some class.

Smooth Ride

The Cadillac V16 was the world's first passenger car with a V16 engine. The engine had a lot of might but ran smoothly.

VOLKSWAGEN BEETLE

Whether you call it a Bug or a Beetle, this is one of the most popular cars in history. It was widely produced after World War II ended in 1945. First called the Volkswagen Type 1, it was later named the Beetle because of its shape. Unlike most cars, the original VW Beetle's engine was in the rear of the car.

1 Draw an oval for the body of the car and three circles for the tires.

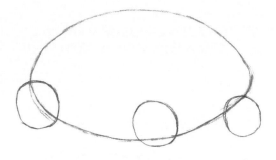

2 Add four small circles for the headlights. Draw shapes for the front windshield and side windows.

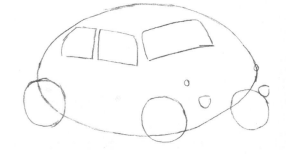

3 Outline the body of the car. Add a side view mirror and a license plate. Then give the tires dimension.

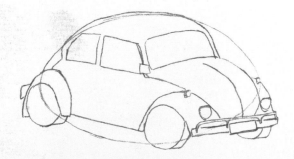

4 Add windshield wipers and a door handle. Give the body its final details.

ART TIP
Add extra designs to the body of your Beetle, like flowers or flames!

5 Outline the finished drawing with a thin, black marker.

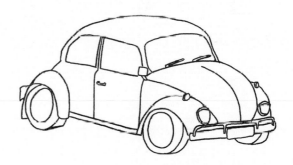

6 Color your Beetle. These cars are often bright and bold, so use your imagination!

Love Bug
In 1968, a Beetle starred in the Disney movie *The Love Bug.* It was a race car named Herbie.

MUSCLE CAR

Vroom vroom vroom! Muscle cars are known for their thunderous engines. Drivers rev them up to show off their "muscle." Muscle cars are ideal for **drag racing**. They were very popular in the United States in the 1960s. Famous models include the Pontiac GTO, the Dodge Charger, and the Shelby Cobra.

1 Draw two ovals for the body of the car and two circles for the tires.

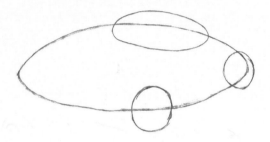

2 Add four small circles for the headlights and one curved rectangle for the windshield.

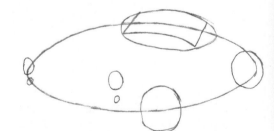

3 Outline the body of the car. Add seats and a steering wheel. Detail the lights and tires.

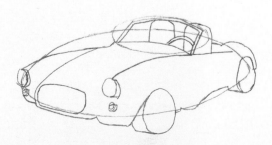

4 Finish detailing the body. Add racing stripes to the hood.

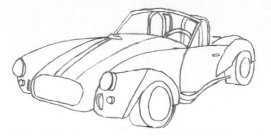

ART TIP
Mix and match different colors for the racing stripes and the body to make your car stand out!

5 Outline the finished drawing with a thin, black marker.

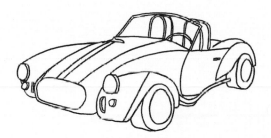

6 Color your car! Red is a classic color for muscle cars, but they come in many colors.

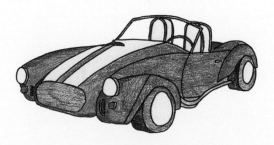

Burnin' Rubber
The 1967 Shelby Cobra's top speed was 165 miles per hour (266 km/h)!

FORMULA ONE CAR

On your mark, get set, go! Formula One (F1) cars are built to reach top speeds as fast as they can. They zoom more than 200 miles per hour (322 km/h) around the racetrack! Formula One cars have an **aerodynamic** shape, lightweight parts, wide tires, and very powerful engines. Drivers wear helmets and sit in open seats.

1 Draw a rectangle for the body of the car and a square for the spoiler. Add four circles for the tires.

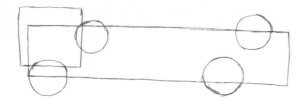

2 Add a driver to the car and a cabin to sit in.

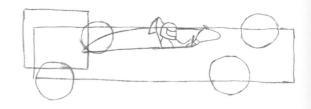

3 Outline the entire car, including the spoiler and front end parts. Give the tires dimension.

4 Add details to the tires and body. Draw the axle that connects the front left tire to the body.

ART TIP

You can make your F1 car look like it's turning just by changing the angle of the shapes.

5 Outline the finished drawing with a thin, black marker.

6 Have fun coloring your F1 car! Draw patterns, designs, words, or anything you want to!

Pit Stop

A "lollypop man" guides a Formula One racer into a pit stop. There, car tires can be changed in less than three seconds!

STOCK CAR

Stock cars are shaped like regular road cars. But don't be fooled! These speedsters are specially built for racing. A stock car's engine packs a punch, allowing it to **accelerate** to up to 200 miles per hour (322 km/h). Most races are held on oval tracks. It may take hours to finish a race. So, drivers must be in good shape.

1 Draw two ovals for the body of the car and two circles for the tires.

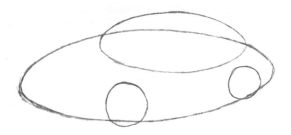

2 Add a rectangle on the back of the larger oval for the spoiler. Draw shapes for the windshield, side windows, and headlights.

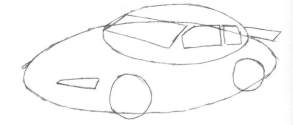

3 Outline the whole car and detail the body.

4 Detail the tires and give this stock car a number so it can race!

ART TIP

Make your car's number a bright color, so the judges can read it when your car crosses the finish line!

5 Outline the finished drawing with a thin, black marker.

6 Color your stock car! These cars are usually bright so they can be seen.

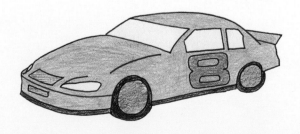

Close Quarters

Stock cars have no doors! Drivers get in and out through the window opening.

17

GREEN CAR

Green cars are environmentally friendly. Cars are a major source of air pollution. In the United States, vehicles produce nearly one-third of the **greenhouse gases** released into the air. To curb that, carmakers build green cars. These include electric cars, such as the Renault Twizy. It runs on a battery that is plugged in to recharge.

1 Draw an oval and a rectangle for the body. Add three circles for tires.

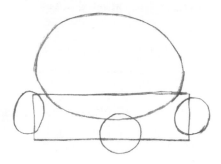

2 Add four small circles for headlights. Draw shapes for the side opening and windshield.

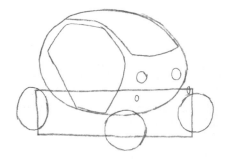

3 Give the tires dimension and add side view mirrors. Outline the entire body of the car.

4 Draw a seat and a steering wheel. Finish detailing the tires.

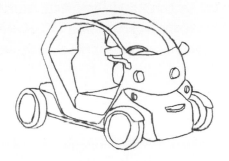

ART TIP

Just drawing a small hint of a steering wheel is all you need to make it look real.

5 Outline the finished drawing with a thin, black marker.

6 Color your green car, or just use black and white!

Vive la France!
Renault is a French car company. Its name is pronounced reh-NOH.

FIRE TRUCK

Red lights flash and a siren blares. A fire truck dashes to an emergency! These large vehicles transport firefighters and their tools. Levers on a fire truck control when water is sprayed from hoses. Some trucks have ladders that extend up to more than 100 feet (30 m) so a firefighter can rescue people from tall buildings.

1 Draw three rectangles for the body and the ladder. Add three circles for the tires.

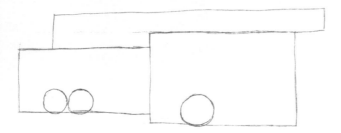

2 Add shapes for the windows and two small squares for the front lights.

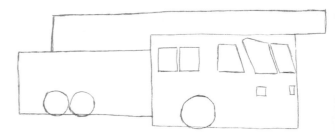

3 Outline the body of the truck, add a side view mirror, and start to detail the ladder.

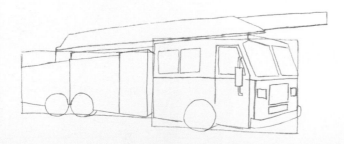

4 Finish the ladder and tires. Add all details to the body, including a stripe.

5 Outline the finished drawing with a thin, black marker.

6 Color this fire truck its famous red color, or use yellow or green!

High Volume

Some fire trucks carry 500 gallons (1,893 L) of water or more! That's about the same as 13 full bathtubs!

DUMP TRUCK

Dump trucks are massive construction machines. Workers use them to move sand, rock, snow, and other heavy materials. A dump truck has a bed, which is filled with material. The driver raises the bed by moving a lever. Then, the truck dumps out its load. Beds of large mining dump trucks can hold more than 300 tons (272 t)!

1 Draw three rectangles for the body of this truck. Add a shape for the front and four circles for the tires.

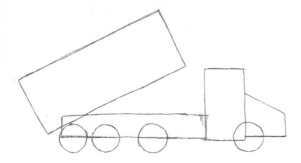

2 Add a side window, details to the body, and a vertical exhaust pipe.

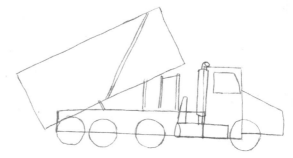

3 Outline the truck. Detail the bed of the truck.

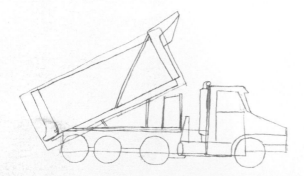

4 Detail the tires, add holes to the exhaust pipe, and add details to the body.

5 Outline the finished drawing with a thin, black marker.

6 Color your dump truck. Most dump trucks have a colored front end and a dull or metal back.

Mighty Movers

The biggest dump trucks measure more than two stories tall! They are so big that their parts have to be shipped to a job site and the trucks are built there.

HUMVEE

Humvees are built to drive over almost any kind of ground. These military vehicles can handle rocks, hills, mud, and even shallow water. The real name for a Humvee is HMMWV, which stands for high **mobility** multipurpose wheeled vehicle. First used by the US Army in 1985, the Humvee often carries troops or weapons.

1 Draw a rectangle for the body and two squares for the front and back. Add three circles for the tires.

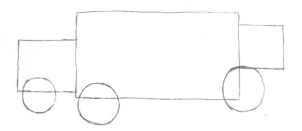

2 Add squares for the windows and four small circles for the headlights.

3 Outline the Humvee, give the tires dimension, and add side view mirrors.

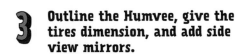

4 Finish the tires and give the body some final detail.

ART TIP

If you shade in your truck windows, they'll look tinted. This gives your drawing a different character.

5 Outline the finished drawing with a thin, black marker.

6 Color your Humvee! Most of these are for the military and are traditional camouflage colors, such as green or tan.

Light but Fast

Humvees look heavy and tough. But they are lightweight and fast.

MONSTER TRUCK

Roar! Crunch! Monster trucks are big and bold. They compete at events so brave drivers can show off a truck's power. Monster trucks jump off ramps, crush cars, and race each other. With massive wheels, a monster truck stands 11 feet (3 m) tall and can weigh 10,000 pounds (4,536 kg) or more!

1 Draw a square and a rectangle for the body. Add four large circles for the tires.

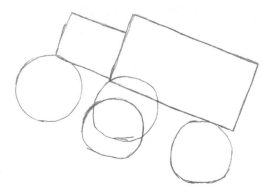

2 Add rectangles for the windshield and side window. Draw two small circles for the headlights. Add lines for the wheel axles and shock absorbers.

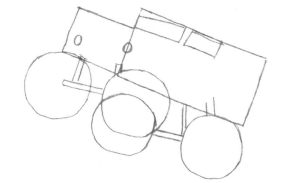

3 Give the tires dimension. Add detail to the wheel axles and shock absorbers. Also outline the entire body.

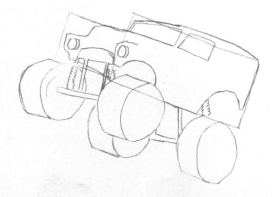

4 Finish the tires, wheel axles, and shock absorbers. Finally, add a skull and crossbones to this monster!

ART TIP

Draw your monster truck at an upward angle to make it look like it's about to take off from a huge jump!

5 Outline the finished drawing with a thin, black marker.

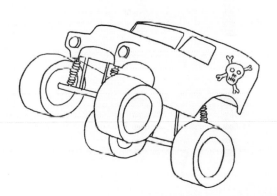

6 Be creative when coloring your monster truck!

Named to Scare

Popular types of monster trucks are the Bigfoot and the Gravedigger.

YOU CAN DRAW!

Fuel for Thought

The first car was built by French engineer Nicolas-Joseph Cugnot in 1769. It ran on steam, not gas!

About 15 percent of the world's passenger cars are in the United States.

About 80 percent of American households own a car. Roughly 35 percent own two or more cars.

Gottlieb Daimler of Germany built the first motor truck in 1896.

In Great Britain, the word for truck is "lorry."

Americans drive about 3 trillion miles (4.8 trillion km) per year. That's the same distance as driving to the sun and back 13,440 times!

Glossary

accelerate (ihk-SEH-luh-rayt) – to increase speed.

aerodynamic (ehr-oh-deye-NA-mihk) – able to move easily through the air.

drag race – a contest where people see whose cars can go the fastest.

equipped (ih-KWIHPT) – supplied with all that is needed.

greenhouse gas – a gas, such as carbon dioxide, that traps heat in Earth's atmosphere.

mobility – the state of being capable of moving easily.

Websites

To learn more about I Like to Draw!, visit **booklinks.abdopublishing.com**. These links are routinely monitored and updated to provide the most current information available.

Index